NINA MILLER

HOW NIGERIANS GOT THEIR INDEPENDENCE

INTRODUCTION

The historical backdrop of Nigeria can be followed to pioneers exchanging across the center East and Africa as soon as 1100 BC. Various old African civic establishments got comfortable the district that is referred to now as Nigeria, for example, the Realm of Nri,the Benin Empire, and the Oyo Empire. Islam arrived at Nigeria through the Bornu Domain between (1068 Promotion) and Hausa States around (1385 Promotion) during the eleventh century,while Christianity came to Nigeria in the fifteenth 100 years through Augustinian and Capuchin priests from Portugal.[citation needed] The Songhai Domain likewise involved piece of the region.From the fifteenth hundred years, European slave dealers showed up in the district to buy oppressed Africans as a component of the Atlantic slave exchange, what began in the area of cutting edge Nigeria; the main Nigerian port utilized by European slave brokers was Badagry, a seaside harbour.

Neighborhood vendors furnished them with slaves, heightening struggles among the ethnic gatherings in the locale and disturbing more seasoned exchange designs through the Trans-Saharan route.

Lagos was involved by English powers in 1851 and officially attached by England in the year 1865. Nigeria turned into an English protectorate in 1901. The time of English rule went on until 1960, when a freedom development prompted the nation being conceded independence.Nigeria previously turned into a republic in 1963, however capitulated to military rule three years after the fact, after a horrendous overthrow. A dissident development later framed the Republic of Biafra in 1967, prompting the three-year Nigerian Common War.Nigeria turned into a republic again after another constitution was written in 1979. In any case, the republic was brief, as the military held onto power again in 1983 and later controlled for a long time. Another republic was wanted to be laid out in 1993, yet was cut short by Broad Sani Abacha. Abacha kicked the bucket in 1998 and a fourth republic was subsequently settled the next year, which finished thirty years of discontinuous military rule.

Who brought freedom to Nigeria?

Inheritance. In 1953, Anthony Enahoro started the self-government movement in the Western Place of Gathering, which in the end prompted Nigerian Freedom on 1 October 1960.

Accordingly, before the name Nigeria was given by Greenery, the whole land under its organization was known as the Regal Niger protectorate.

Chapter 1

Prehistory

Archeological exploration, spearheaded by Charles Thurstan Shaw, has shown a long history of human settlement in Nigeria. Unearthings in Ugwuele, Afikpo and Nsukka show proof of residence as soon as 6,000 BC.Shaw's unearthings at Igbo-Ukwu uncovered a ninth century native culture that made exceptionally refined work in bronze metalworking, free of Middle Easterner or European impact and hundreds of years before different destinations that were better known at the hour of discovery.

The earliest known illustration of a fossil human skeleton found anyplace in West Africa, which is 13,000 years of age, was found at Iwo-Eleru in Isarun, western Nigeria, and validates the vestige of residence in the region.

The Dufuna kayak was found in 1987 not a long way from the

Komadugu Gana Stream, in Yobe State.Radiocarbon dating of an example of charcoal found close to the site dates the kayak at 8,500 to 8,000 years of age, connecting the site to Lake Mega Chad. It is the most seasoned boat found in Africa, and the second most seasoned known worldwide.

Stone hatchet heads, imported in extraordinary amounts from the north and utilized in opening the woods for agrarian turn of events, were loved by the Yoruba relatives of Neolithic trailblazers as "thunderclaps" flung to earth by the gods.

Nok Culture and early Iron Age

Alter

Primary article: Nok culture

The Nok culture flourished from roughly 1,500 BC to around 200 Promotion on the Jos Level in north and focal Nigeria and delivered life-sized earthenware figures that incorporate human heads, human figures, and animals. Iron refining heaters at Taruga, a Nok site, date from around 600 BC. The Nok culture is remembered to have started purifying iron by 600-500 BC and potentially a few centuries earlier. Kainji Dam unearthings uncovered iron-working by the second century BC. Proof of iron refining has likewise been uncovered at destinations in the Nsukka locale of southeast Nigeria in the thing is currently Igboland: dating to 2,000 BC at the site of Lejja and to 750 BC at the site of Opi. The change from Neolithic times to the Iron Age obviously was accomplished natively without moderate bronze creation. Others have recommended that the innovation moved west from the Nile Valley, albeit the Iron Age in the Niger Waterway valley and the woods locale seems to originate before the presentation of metallurgy in the upper savanna by over 800 years. The earliest iron innovation in West Africa has likewise been viewed as contemporary with or originate before that of the Nile valley and North Africa, and a few archeologists accept that iron metallurgy was reasonable grown freely in sub-Saharan West Africa.

chapter 2

Early states before 1500

The early autonomous realms and states that make up present-day province of Nigeria are (in sequential request): Benin Realm, Borgu Realm, Fulani Domain, Hausa Realms, Kanem Bornu Realm, Kwararafa Realm, Ibibio Realm, Nri Realm, Nupe Realm, Oyo Realm, Songhai Domain, Warri Realm, Ile Ife Realm, and Yagba East Realm.

Oyo and Benin

Alter

Principal article: Oyo Domain

During the fifteenth century Oyo and Benin outperformed Ife as political and financial powers, despite the fact that Ife protected its status as a strict focus. Regard for the consecrated elements of the oni of Ife was a vital calculate the development of Yoruba culture. The Ife model of government was adjusted at Oyo, where an individual from its decision line controlled a few more modest city-states. A state gathering (the Oyo Mesi) named the

Alaafin (lord) and went about as a mind his position. Their capital city was arranged around 100 km north of present-day Oyo. Not at all like the woodland bound Yoruba realms, Oyo was in the savanna and drew its tactical strength from its rangers powers, which laid out authority over the nearby Nupe and the Borgu realms and in this manner created shipping lanes farther toward the north.

The Benin Domain (1440-1897; called Bini by local people) was a pre-pioneer African state in what is currently current Nigeria. It ought not be mistaken for the current nation called Benin, previously called Dahomey.

Fundamental article: Benin Realm

The Igala are an ethnic gathering of Nigeria. Their country, the previous Igala Realm, is a roughly three-sided area of around 14,000 km2 (5,400 sq mi) in the point shaped by the Benue and Niger waterways. The region was previously the Igala Division of Kabba territory, and is currently essential for Kogi State. The capital is Idah in Kogi state. Igala individuals are significantly found in Kogi state. They can be found in Idah, Igalamela/Odolu, Ajaka, Ofu, Olamaboro, Dekina, Bassa, Ankpa, omala, Lokoja, Ibaji, Ajaokuta, Lokoja and kotonkarfe Nearby government all in Kogi state. Different states where Igalas can be found are Anambra, Delta and Benue states. The illustrious stool of Olu of warri was established by an Igala sovereign.

Primary article: History of Nigeria (1500-1800)

Savanna states

Alter

During the sixteenth 100 years, the Songhai Realm arrived at its pinnacle, extending from the Senegal and Gambia waterways and consolidating part of Hausaland in the east. Simultaneously the Saifawa Line of Borno vanquished Kanem and stretched out control west to Hausa urban communities not under Songhai authority. Generally due to Songhai's impact, there was a blooming of Islamic learning and culture. Songhai imploded in 1591 when a Moroccan armed force vanquished Gao and Timbuktu. Morocco couldn't handle the realm and the different regions, including the Hausa states, became free. The breakdown sabotaged Songhai's authority over the Hausa states and suddenly modified the direction of provincial history.

Borno arrived at its apex under mai Idris Aloma (ca. 1569-1600) during whose rule Kanem was reconquered. The annihilation of Songhai left Borno uncontested and until the eighteenth century Borno ruled northern Nigeria. Regardless of Borno's authority the Hausa states kept on wrestling for domination. Steadily Borno's position debilitated; its powerlessness to actually take a look at political contentions between contending Hausa urban communities was one illustration of this decay. Another component was the tactical danger of the Tuareg focused at Agades who entered the northern regions of Borno.

The significant reason for Borno's decay was an extreme dry spell that struck the Sahel and savanna from in the eighteenth hundred years. As a result, Borno lost numerous northern regions to the Tuareg whose portability permitted them to successfully persevere through the starvation more. Borno recovered a portion of its previous could in the succeeding many years, yet one more dry season happened during the 1790s, again debilitating the state.

Natural and political insecurity gave the foundation to the jihad of Usman dan Fodio. The tactical contentions of the Hausa states stressed the locale's monetary assets when dry spell and starvation subverted ranchers and herders. Numerous Fulani moved into Hausaland and Borno, and their appearance expanded pressures since they had no devotion to the political specialists, who considered them to be a wellspring of expanded tax collection. Toward the finish of the eighteenth hundred years, some Muslim ulema started articulating the complaints of the average citizens. Endeavors to wipe out or control these strict pioneers just elevated the pressures, making way for jihad.

As per the Reference book of African History, "It is assessed that by the 1890s the biggest slave populace of the world, around 2 million individuals, was gathered in the domains of the Sokoto Caliphate. The utilization of slave work was broad, particularly in agriculture.

Chapter 3

Hausa Kingdoms

The Hausa Realms were an assortment of states began by the Hausa public, arranged between the Niger Waterway and Lake Chad. Their set of experiences is reflected in the Bayajidda legend, which portrays the undertakings of the Baghdadi legend Bayajidda finishing in the killing of the snake in the well of Daura and the marriage with the nearby sovereign magajiya Daurama. While the legend had a kid with the sovereign, Bawo, and one more kid with the sovereign's house keeper worker, Karbagari.

Sarki folklore

Alter

As per the Bayajidda legend, the Hausa states were established by the children of Bayajidda, a ruler whose beginning contrasts by custom, however official ordinance records him as the individual who wedded the last Kabara of Daura and proclaimed the finish of the matriarchal rulers that had past governed

the Hausa people.
Contemporary verifiable grant sees this legend as a moral story like numerous around there of Africa that presumably referred to a significant occasion, like a change in administering lines.

Banza Bakwai

Alter

As indicated by the Bayajidda legend, the Banza Bakwai states were established by the seven children of Karbagari ("Town-seizer"), the exceptional child of Bayajidda and the slave-house keeper, Bagwariya. They are known as the Banza Bakwai meaning Jerk or Fake Seven because of their ancestress' slave status.

Zamfara (state possessed by Hausa-speakers)

Kebbi (state possessed by Hausa-speakers)

Yauri (likewise called Yawuri)

Gwari (additionally called Gwariland)

Kwararafa (the condition of the Jukun public)

Nupe (condition of the Nupe public)

Ilorin(was established by the Yoruba)

Hausa Bakwai

Alter

The Hausa Realms started as seven states established by the Bayajidda legend by the six children of Bawo, the remarkable child of the legend and the sovereign Magajiya Daurama notwithstanding the legend's child, Biram or Ibrahim, of a prior marriage. The states included just realms possessed by Hausa-speakers:

Daura:

Kano:

Katsina

Zaria (Zazzau)

Gobir

Rano

Biram:

Chapter 4

Yoruba

By and large, the Yoruba public have been the prevailing gathering on the west bank of the Niger. Their closest semantic family members are the Igala who live on the contrary side of the Niger's disparity from the Benue, and from whom they are accepted to have divided around quite a while back. The Yoruba were coordinated in for the most part patrilineal gatherings that involved town networks and stayed alive on farming. From roughly the eighth 100 years, adjoining town compounds called ile mixed into various regional city-states in which faction loyalties became subordinate to dynastic chieftains. Urbanization was joined by elevated degrees of imaginative accomplishment, especially in earthenware and ivory mold and in the refined metal projecting delivered at Ife.

The Yoruba are particularly known for the Oyo Domain that overwhelmed the district. The Oyo Realm held matchless quality over other Yoruba countries like the Egba Realm, Awori Realm, and the Egbado. Thriving, they likewise overwhelmed the Realm of Dahomey (presently situated in the advanced Republic of Benin).

The Yoruba honor a pantheon made out of a Preeminent God, Olorun and the Orisha. The Olorun is currently called God in the Yoruba language. There are 400 divinities called Orisha who perform different tasks. As indicated by the Yoruba, Oduduwa is viewed as the predecessor of the Yoruba lords. As per one of the different fantasies about him, he established Ife and dispatched his children and girls to lay out comparable realms in different pieces of what is today known as Yorubaland. The Yorubaland presently comprises of various clans from various states which are situated in the Southwestern piece of the nation, states like Lagos State, Oyo State, Ondo State, Osun State, Ekiti State and Ogun State, among others.

Chapter 5

A British sphere of influence

Following the Napoleonic Conflicts, the English extended exchange with the Nigerian inside. In 1885, English cases to a West African effective reach got global acknowledgment; and in the next year, the Illustrious Niger Organization was sanctioned under the initiative of Sir George Taubman Goldie. On the 31st of December 1899 the contract for the Illustrious Niger Organization was repudiated by the English government, and the amount of £865,000 was paid to the organization as remuneration. The whole region of the Illustrious Niger Organization came under the control of the English government. On 1 January 1900, the English Domain made the Southern Nigeria Protectorate and the Northern Nigeria Protectorate.

In 1914, the region was officially joined as the State and Protectorate of Nigeria. Authoritatively, Nigeria stayed partitioned into the Northern and Southern Territories and Lagos Colony. Western schooling and the improvement of a cutting edge economy continued more quickly in the south than in the north, with results felt in Nigeria's political life from that point forward. Following The Second Great War, in light of the development of Nigerian patriotism and requests for freedom, progressive constitutions enacted by the English government pushed Nigeria toward self-government on a delegate and progressively bureaucratic premise. On 1 October 1954, the province turned into the independent Alliance of Nigeria. By the center of the twentieth hundred years, the incredible wave for freedom was clearing across Africa. On 27 October 1958 England concurred that Nigeria would turn into a free state on 1 October 1960.

Chapter 6

Independence

The League of Nigeria was conceded full freedom on 1 October 1960 under a constitution that accommodated a parliamentary government and a significant proportion of self-government for the country's three districts. From 1959 to 1960, Jaja Wachuku was the Main Nigerian Speaker of the Nigerian Parliament, additionally called the "Place of Agents." Jaja Wachuku supplanted Sir

Frederick Metcalfe of England. Outstandingly, as First Speaker of the House, Jaja Wachuku accepted Nigeria's Instrument of Autonomy, otherwise called Opportunity Sanction, on 1 October 1960, from Princess Alexandra of Kent, the Sovereign's delegate at the Nigerian freedom functions. Sovereign Elizabeth II was ruler of Nigeria and head of state, and Nigeria was an individual from the English Ward of Countries. The Central government was given selective powers in safeguard, unfamiliar relations, and business and monetary strategy. The ruler of Nigeria was still head of state yet regulative power was vested in a bicameral parliament, leader power in a state leader and bureau, and legal expert in a Government High Court. Ideological groups, notwithstanding, would in general mirror the cosmetics of the three primary ethnic gatherings. The Northern Nation's Congress (NPC) addressed moderate, Muslim, generally Hausa and Fulani intrigues that overwhelmed the northern district of the nation, comprising of 3/4 of the land region and the greater part the number of inhabitants in Nigeria. In this manner the North ruled the league government from the outset of autonomy. In the 1959 races held in anticipation of freedom, the NPC caught 134 seats in the 312-seat parliament.

Catching 89 seats in the government parliament was the second-biggest party in the recently autonomous country the Public Chamber of Nigerian Residents (NCNC). The NCNC addressed the interests of the Igbo-and Christian-ruled individuals of the Eastern Locale of Nigeria. and the Activity Gathering (AG) was a left-inclining party that addressed the interests of the Yoruba nation in the West. In the 1959 races, the AG got 73 seats.

The primary post-freedom public government was framed by a moderate coalition of the NCNC and the NPC. Upon freedom, it was broadly expected that Ahmadu Bello the Sardauna of Sokoto, the undisputed resilient man in Nigeria who controlled the North, would become State head of the new League Government. Notwithstanding, Bello decided to stay as chief of the North and as party manager of the NPC, chose Sir Abubakar Tafawa Balewa, a Hausa, to turn into Nigeria's most memorable Head of the state.

The Yoruba-overwhelmed AG turned into the resistance under its alluring chief Boss Obafemi Awolowo. Nonetheless, in 1962, a group emerged inside the AG under the initiative of Ladoke Akintola who had been chosen as chief of the West. The Akintola group contended that the Yoruba people groups were losing their pre-famous situation in business in Nigeria to individuals of the Igbo clan in light of the fact that the Igbo-ruled NCNC was important for the administering alliance and the AG was not. The central government Top state leader, Balewa concurred with the Akintola group and tried to have the AG join the public authority.

The party administration under Awolowo differ and supplanted Akintola as head of the West with one of their own allies. In any case, when the Western District parliament met to endorse this change, Akintola allies in the parliament began an uproar in the offices of the parliament. Battling between the individuals broke out. Seats were tossed and one part gotten the parliamentary Mace and used it like a weapon to go after the Speaker and different individuals. At last, the police with poisonous gas were expected to control the mob. In resulting endeavors to reconvene the Western parliament, comparable aggravations broke out. Agitation went on in the West and added toward the Western Locale's standing for, viciousness, rebellion and manipulated elections. Central Government State leader Balewa proclaimed military regulation in the Western District and captured Awolowo and different individuals from his group accused them of conspiracy. Akintola was selected to head an alliance government in the Western Locale. Accordingly, the AG was diminished to a resistance job in their own stronghold.

chapter 7

Democracy Day

Nigeria's Majority rules government day was initially praised on May 29, consistently since General Olusegun Obasanjo arose President in 1999. Nonetheless, on June 12, 2018, General Muhammadu Buhari, as president, reported a change in this date from May 29 to June 12, as from the year 2019. This was to honor the June twelfth appointment of 1993, and the occasions that encompassed it.

www.ingramcontent.com/pod-product-compliance
Lightning Source LLC
LaVergne TN
LVHW050011170826
845677LV00023B/3867

* 9 7 9 8 3 5 5 8 2 6 7 3 4 *